SERENA WILLIAMS

by Elizabeth Raum

AMICUS HIGH INTEREST • AMICUS INK

Amicus High Interest and Amicus Ink are imprints of Amicus
P.O. Box 1329, Mankato, MN 56002
www.amicuspublishing.us

Library of Congress Cataloging-in-Publication Data
Names: Raum, Elizabeth, author.
Title: Serena Williams / by Elizabeth Raum.
Description: Mankato, Minnesota : Amicus, 2018. | Series: Amicus High
 Interest. Pro Sports Biographies | Includes index. | Audience: K to Grade 3.
Identifiers: LCCN 2016058343 (print) | LCCN 2017000380 (ebook) | ISBN
 9781681511399 (library binding) | ISBN 9781681521701 (pbk.) | ISBN
 9781681512297 (ebook)
Subjects: LCSH: Williams, Serena, 1981---Juvenile literature. | African
 American women tennis players--Biography--Juvenile literature. |
 Women tennis players--United States--Biography--Juvenile literature.
Classification: LCC GV994.W55 R38 2018 (print) | LCC GV994.W55 (ebook) |
 DDC 796.342092 [B] --dc23
LC record available at
 https://lccn.loc.gov/2016058343

Photo Credits: William West/AFP cover; Juergen Hasenkopf/REX/
Shutterstock 2, 12–13; Ben Curtis/AP/REX/Shutterstock 4–5, 22;
Ken Levine/Getty Images 7; Bob Thomas/Getty Images 8–9; Diand
Bondareff/AP/REX/Shutterstock 11; Cedric Weber/
Alamy 14–15; Reuters/Alamy Stock Photo 16–17;
Pongmanat Tasiri/EPA/Newscom 19; Elise
Amendola/AP/REX/Shutterstock 20–21

Editor: Wendy Dieker
Designer: Aubrey Harper
Photo Researcher: Holly Young

Printed in the United States of America

HC 10 9 8 7 6 5 4 3 2 1
PB 10 9 8 7 6 5 4 3 2 1

TABLE OF CONTENTS

Game On   5

Early Start   6

Going Pro   9

Grand Slam   10

Golden Slam   13

A Sister Team   14

Helping Kids   17

Fashionista   18

The Best   21

Just the Facts   22

Words to Know   23

Learn More   24

Index   24

GAME ON

Serena Williams steps onto the tennis court. She tosses the tennis ball into the air. Smack! It's a perfect **serve**. Williams' perfect serve has made her a tennis star.

EARLY START

Williams was born in Michigan. When she was three, her family moved to California. Her sister Venus was five. Their dad taught them to play tennis. They practiced two hours a day.

Serena is the youngest of five sisters. Only she and Venus play tennis.

GOING PRO

At age 10, Williams was the best player her age in the United States. The family moved to Florida. Williams joined the Women's Tennis Association (WTA) when she was 14.

GRAND SLAM

By 2002, Williams was the best **singles** player in the world. In 2003, she won a **Grand Slam**. This means she won the four top WTA **tournaments** in a row.

The Grand Slam tournaments are the Australian Open, French Open, Wimbledon, and US Open.

GOLDEN SLAM

In 2012, Williams won the singles Olympic gold medal. Before the next Olympics, she won a Grand Slam again. People call this a Career Golden Slam.

A SISTER TEAM

Williams also plays **doubles** with Venus. They win. They have not lost a Grand Slam match together. They also won three Olympic gold medals together.

The Williams sisters have also gone head-to-head in singles many times. Serena usually wins.

HELPING KIDS

Williams earns lots of money when she wins tennis matches. She uses her money to help others. Many kids around the world don't have schools. She gave money to build schools in Kenya.

FASHIONISTA

Williams also loves fashion. She **designs** clothes. Models wear her designs. Williams brings her style to the tennis court, too. She wears bright colors and fun prints.

THE BEST

Williams has not always been the top player. Even still, she won 10 ESPY awards. ESPN named her "Best Female Tennis Player" eight times and "Best Female Athlete" twice. She will always be known as one of the best.

JUST THE FACTS

Born: September 26, 1981

Hometown: Saginaw, Michigan

Joined the pros: 1995

Stats: www.wtatennis.com/players/player/9044/title/serena-williams

Accomplishments:

- Singles Tournament Grand Slams: 2003, 2015

- Career Golden Slam: 2015

- Olympic Gold medals: 1 singles, 3 doubles

- Earned the most career wins in the four Grand Slam tournaments: 2017 (23 wins)

- ESPY award for Best Female Tennis Player: 2003, 2004, 2009, 2010, 2011, 2013, 2015, 2016

- Season-ending rank of #1: 2002, 2009, 2013, 2014, 2015

WORDS TO KNOW

design – to plan and sketch an outfit or piece of clothing

doubles – a tennis game played by teams of two

Grand Slam – when a tennis player or team wins the four Grand Slam tournaments (Australian Open, French Open, Wimbledon, and US Open) in a row

singles – a tennis game played one-on-one

serve – to hit the ball over the net to start a tennis play

tournament – a series of matches or games where winners advance to the next round and losers are eliminated

LEARN MORE

Read More

Gagne, Tammy. *Day by Day with Serena Williams*. Hockessin, Del.: Mitchell Lane Publishers, 2016.

Kortemeier, Todd. *Superstars of Pro Tennis*. Mankato, Minn.: Amicus, 2016.

Websites

Serena Williams | ESPN
http://www.espn.com/tennis/player/_/id/394/serena-williams

Tennis Facts for Kids
http://tennisfactsforkids.weebly.com/tennis-rules.html

INDEX

doubles 14

ESPN awards 21

fashion 18

going pro 9
Grand Slam 10, 13

helping others 17

Olympics 13, 14

serving 5
singles 10, 13, 14

training 6

Williams, Venus 6, 14